HAVING FAITH IN THE FACE OF UNCERTAINTY

HAVING FAITH IN THE FACE OF UNCERTAINTY

Reflections on Brenton's Early Arrival

Nicholas A. Meade

Foreword by Tanesha R. Meade

Title: Having Faith in the Face of Uncertainty: Reflections on Brenton's Early Arrival
Copyright © 2015 Nicholas A. Meade Ministries

Cover Art By:
The Church Online
thechurchonline.com

All rights reserved. No part of this publication may be reproduced, distributed, or transmitted in any form or by any means, including photocopying, recording, or other electronic or mechanical methods, without the prior written permission of the publisher, except in the case of brief quotations embodied in critical reviews and certain other noncommercial uses permitted by copyright law.

For permission requests, send an email to the publisher with the subject line "Copyright Permissions" to the following email address:
    Nicholas A. Meade Ministries
    publishing@nicholasmeade.com
    www.nicholasmeade.com

Library of Congress Control Number: 2015919232

ISBN 978-0-9861654-2-9

Contents

Foreword	vi
Preface	ix
Acknowledgements	xi
Dedication	xiii
A Letter to My Son	xiv
1 The Journey toward Fatherhood	1
2 The Disheartening Incorrect Diagnosis	13
3 The Mistaken Gender Prediction	26
4 Preparing for Brenton's Arrival	38
5 Brenton Arrives Prematurely	50
6 The Hospital Journeys	61
7 The Long-Awaited Home Arrival	71
8 The Brenton We Know Now	80
Appendix: The Pictures	86

FOREWORD

Wrapping your head around the fact that *you* will be having a child can build a surmounting level of uncertainty for any parent. Coming to terms with knowing *you* will be a parent is a separate "coming to terms" all in itself. *Having Faith in the Face of Uncertainty* uncovers the vulnerability we have as human beings first, and secondly as people of faith. In this book, my husband Dr. Nicholas Meade makes visible to the reader the many hats he wore during this very trying time in our lives. As a new husband, new father, and a new minister there was always an expectation of how he should respond in dealing with the disheartening premature birth of our son and all of the medical setbacks he encountered. The refreshing approach Nicholas takes in this book is to expose his vulnerabilities as being human first, especially when he had no solutions or answers to the problems that he faced. Brenton's journey parallels the growth in my husband's faith. Looking back, Brenton's birthweight of only two and a half pounds symbolized the type of faith that Luke 17:6 refers to as a *mustard seed*. When uncertainty lingers longer then we expect with no answers from God in sight our humanity can come to a crossroads: We can continue to look to God, we can rely on our own understanding, or we can wallow in despair. It can be a struggle for people of faith to keep up appearances, but God honors a relationship when we can come just as we are, insecurities and all. Nicholas discloses how people of faith can become comfortable knowing God's history of what God has done for us in one area of our lives. However when God tests us in a new area we can be assured that the ground is now fertile for new growth in our lives. When this occurs we can sit back and marvel at how much that once mustard seed is on its way to provide shade to cover us.

Having Faith in the Face of Uncertainty is a wonderful account of how we can become overconfident in ones' own faith only for God to expose areas in our lives in need of nourishment, but it also is valuable in exposing the treasure of self-reflection and seeing God's hand at work when initially it seemed invisible. The human condition is unique to every individual but encouragement can always be drawn from becoming aware of the mental and physical struggles we face. This individual account my husband experienced is a true gem for people of faith, and hopefully it will inspire you to tell your story.

Tanesha R. Meade
Brenton's Mom

Preface

Having Faith in the Face of Uncertainty came into being as the result of my faith journey after welcoming my premature son Brenton. I wanted to write this book to share all of the moments in this journey where God demonstrated God's presence and concern about our struggle. The more I looked back on those times the more I saw God's hands in our situation. Therefore it is my heart's desire that through this book someone may be inspired to not only embrace God but also to be encouraged if one finds him or herself in a similar situation.

Years after Brenton's birth, my uncle by marriage asked me to speak with one of his deacons who had just welcomed his own son into the world prematurely. Weeks later I learned that speaking with him helped him to endure the trial of his experience. My hope is that as it was with this father, this book inspires and encourages other parents of premature children not only so that they can keep persevering no matter where they are in their journey but so that one day they will document their own story for the benefit of someone else. I pray that Brenton's story blesses each reader of this book and that it edifies the reader's faith in God and confidence that the reader can overcome anything.

ACKNOWLEDGEMENTS

    I would like to utilize this space to praise God for this finished work. God deserves the glory for bringing us through the challenging times that enable us to now look back through the lenses of faith and see God's hands at work. I also must acknowledge the minds and hearts of those who helped me finish this work including my reader Dr. Lori D. Spears.

    When it comes to Brenton's story I must express our thanks to everyone who helped us along the way. To all of the many healthcare professionals who aided or assisted with my son's care (at Harbor Hospital, Johns Hopkins Hospital, and Mt. Washington Pediatric Hospital) and who took the time to explain things to us and calm our anxieties: thank you. To the service oriented professionals such as those in Maryland's Infants and Toddlers Program who worked with my son to ensure no cognitive lags or developmental delays: thank you.

To my church family, including Pastor Jesse Young, who visited with us and prayed with us throughout the ordeal and even to this day, thank you for everything. To his godparents Chalia Belt and Dr. Robert E. Young, thank you for your influence and earning our trust with our first child. To the many extended family members and our parents who welcomed their first grandson, thank you for your unwavering support and kindness!

To my wife, with whom I travelled this journey, I want to say thank you for bringing our first child into the world. Thank you also for being the best partner in parenting I could ever hope to have. We have overcome so much but I truly do believe as evidenced in Brenton's story that with God walking with us the best is yet to come.

DEDICATION

    This work is dedicated to every parent of a child born prematurely and for those who love them. This book is also dedicated to my son for prayerfully winning the hardest fight he will have to face. This book is dedicated to my wife whose strength helped me and for being the type of mother that a father dreams about having has a helpmate.

A Letter to My Son

Brenton,

This book tells the story of how you have already overcome so much. You are already a survivor! This is a testimony to the God who saw you through all of it and who helped us to endure so that we were right by your side. Let this book shine a light on the greatness of your story. Given all that you have already overcome, do not let anything or anyone stand in the way of you accomplishing what God has for you. No matter what is placed in front of you do not allow yourself to become intimidated. You will face many more obstacles between now and the end of your story because of who you are and because of what you are. But let your past teach you that with God you can overcome anything.

Words cannot adequately express how much we love you and thank God for you. We have watched you overcome your obstacles and turn into a great young man with amazing possibilities. You are already a great big brother, a dedicated student, and a gifted musician. Do not lose sight of these things. Your mother and I want nothing less than for you to surpass what we have accomplished. The good news is that for you, my son, the sky is the limit. Thank you for being the son that you already are. Thank you in advance for the man that you will become. Your story blesses us still and I hope it blesses others. When your children and your children's children read this story they will likewise marvel at how much you overcame. I am proud of you and proud to call you my son. This is from your father: you are my beloved son, in whom I am well pleased.

-Dad

Now faith is the assurance of things hoped for, the conviction of things not seen.

– Hebrews 11:1 NRSV

1

THE JOURNEY TOWARD FATHERHOOD

In my earliest days, the thought of fatherhood rarely crossed my mind. While I believed that I wanted three children where my lone daughter would be sandwiched between two sons, serving as a father did not seem to be a top priority. Perhaps like others I knew that naturally after getting married the most logical step was to pursue starting a family with my wife. However, I failed to take the time to look far into the future beyond our wedding once we became engaged early Christmas morning in 2003. Brenton's story never would have been started had not my wife and I reconnected after breaking up in high school. Not only does the Bible testify of God's ability to bring people back from the dead but I am a witness that God can resurrect dead relationships once we stand ready to steward them faithfully.

On one morning in January 2002 while home on my winter break from the University of Maryland, I did a morning devotion where I meditated on God and prayed. While in this state, the name of my wife Tanesha suddenly came to mind. Even though then it seemed random, in hindsight I see that it was actually an answer to my prayers. Being fed up with the dating dance and being introverted made me a cynic when it came to getting involved in relationships. I grew tired of every lead failing to pan out especially after praying and explicitly asking for God's favor in trying to establish a relationship with some women. These failures taught me that God knows how to say no even when we ask for something we greatly desire. God knows what's best for us because God is the one who has what's best for us. Oftentimes we block ourselves and sabotage what God has for us because we settle for what Dr. John Kinney would call "less than God's best."

Frustrated with the way things were, I approached God in exasperation and asked God to give me who God had for me. It was on the heels of this request that her name dropped in my mind during this morning devotion. God knows how to answer your prayers and meet your need in God's own time! For some reason, upon hearing her name I mentally traced the route to her house from my house. One of the things with which God has gifted me is a photographic memory. Since God knows the future as God knows the past, God's hindsight is just as perfect as God's foresight—God's photographic memory is just as vivid as God's photographic projections. God knows vividly where we have been and where we are going. It only makes sense to trust God not just with our past, and our now but also with our not yet.

The next morning, I awoke to a private message in my Black Planet account from my now wife Tanesha who said she saw me on the system and thought that she would reach out and say hello. Imagine that! The day after God speaks her name to me, she reaches out to me on the system. God does all things well! I realized that I needed to follow up on this and so I responded. We went back and forth a couple of times before agreeing to speak on the phone. For the first time in five years we then spoke on the phone for four hours and it was as if no time had passed. What was clear after our conversation is that while we still were drawn to each other, both of us matured over the years and were in a better place to handle a serious relationship. This helped me to see that God knows how to withhold what you need until you can handle it. God knew that I had not handled our prior relationship the right way so God waited until I could.

Five years prior, after a pregnancy scare, I ended our relationship because I did not want to forfeit my future by having to raise a child I was not ready to receive. The relationship had to be destroyed not because of any wrong doings on her part, but because I feared the consequences of my lack of self-control. Fear, in this case, gave me such pause that I preferred misery over making repeated mistakes. While often demonized, fear by itself is not a negative or counterintuitive to faith. Fear is only a negative if it leads you away from God. If you recall the story of Jesus on the boat when the boat is about to sink they asked if Jesus cared that they were perishing. Their fear of the consequences drove them to turn to Christ just as fear should cause us to do the same.

Upon reconnecting with Tanesha, I had another chance to do right by this woman who I loved. God granted me a second chance to get right what I got wrong the first time. This is the kind of God that I serve! God grants multiple chances and trusts us again with what we destroyed because God knows we can handle it better once we mature. I praise God for my second chance with this wonderful woman. This time I determined to do what was right and would not let her get away. On our second first date it felt like old times. Surely sometimes God allows us to partner with what is familiar on our journey to experiencing the unfamiliar. God knows who you need with you to walk with you to get where God wants you to go.

Our love affair reached a milestone when on the shores of Grand Bahama Island we exchanged vows in front of family and friends. It felt like a formality had finally been settled. We reconnected as a couple in January 2002 after being apart for five years and we knew within a month of our reconciliation that we would one day be married. We both had some growing to do and some maturing to do before we were fit to commit ourselves to one another. In a way it reminds me of the story of Moses where Moses knew what he wanted to do but he grew for forty years before actually being privileged to serve God's people. God knows what types of processes it will take and how long to let us experience the effects of life's crucible in order for us to be better suited for what lies ahead.

The morning after our wedding, while many of our guests prepared to leave and others prepared to enjoy the island for several days, I and my wife headed to the airport for an early flight to neighboring Nassau. As we sat in the airport waiting for our flight to board suddenly I had the epiphany that caught my wife by surprise. I told her that maybe it would not be the worst thing to have children sooner rather than later. Previously we discussed putting off having children so that we could get used to being married and spending time with each other before the interrupting sound of the cries of children.

An explanation for the sudden shift escapes me, but I do know that what happened to me reflects the truth that God knows how to get you comfortable with some ideas with which you formerly were opposed. There was a time where I could not imagine being a father, a preacher, or a student having earned both masters and doctorate degrees but God got me comfortable with the idea. God knows how to move the compass of our hearts desires in God's desired direction slowly but surely. God can do this in part because God always knows what is best and knows our future like the past.

So here we were, not even twenty-four hours removed from marriage, and we were discussing starting a family. Accomplishing one great thing did not prevent us from surveying our lives to identify what might come next. Invariably, after critical accomplishments in our lives we need to have the faith and courage to ask God "what next?" Before I graduated with my Master of Divinity degree I wondered what next so much so that a month prior to crossing the stage with my degree I had already applied and been accepted to the doctoral program at United Theological Seminary. We have to grow to the place where we not only enjoy where we are right now but we are also hopeful enough to ask God "what next?" We can do this when we remember that it was God who walked with us from back then until now so surely God can walk with us from our now until our not yet.

The year 2005 turned out to be a banner year for us and this included our marriage in the place of our dreams. In addition, I secured a higher-paying job that was closer to home. Originally out of college, I worked for a company in northern Virginia that would oftentimes produce commutes of one and a half hours each way. This lengthy commute served as a blessing and a curse. It served as a curse in the sense that I was so far from home and it was an on-call position that even necessitated my coming in to work on the Christmas morning after we became engaged. The blessing, however, was that I was able to worship, praise, and meditate on my way to and or from work. It is absolutely true that sometimes God isolates us for extended periods of time by putting us in positions so as to secure quality time with God. My new position was about twenty minutes from our home. This taught me the valuable lesson that sometimes we need to sojourn through struggle on our way to the better that God has for us.

In the same year, we also purchased our first home. After spending a few months living in my wife's parent's home after our nuptials, we moved into our new home in October of 2005. This home was a four-level townhome with three ample sized bedrooms. We chose this home not simply because of its impressive master suite but also because we had the room that we would need to expand our family one day. This reminds me that in making plans for the future and when walking with God we need to allow room for God to bless us. At the time I could not imagine that not even ten years later those two bedrooms would house four innocent souls. God enabled us to own our home much sooner than our parents and many others that we knew. This makes sense given the fact that God is a master of time and timetables. God knows how to put us in positions to do both what others have not done or to be able to do what others have done sooner. This does not mean that we are somehow superior to those who have come before us but it is a reminder that we stand on the shoulders of many.

In contradistinction to our timetable for home ownership, we actually married and began having children at an age later than that of our parents. About three months after moving into our home, we conceived. My mind still houses the memory of how we suspected that my wife was pregnant and so, like any good husband, I visited the local pharmacy to pick up the best pregnancy test I could find. While cheaper tests would have been sufficient, I did not want any mistakes or false positives. I remember her taking the test and us waiting for the result to show on the test. Imagine how it feels to want something so badly and then have to wait in this moment for two minutes or so to discover if you have reason to be excited about how that for which you have waited is finally here! That is how I felt as my wife handed me the test with a slight smirk on her face that I could not discern. As I glanced down and saw in plain English the word "Pregnant" I could not help but beam with joy. The moment was here. My wife then in so many words blamed me for the fact that it did not take very long for her to get pregnant. This was in spite of our removal of hindrances to getting pregnant in the form of birth control. What do I say about all of this? Perhaps this teaches us that when you remove that which was blocking conception, you can indeed become pregnant with a blessing.

It would be remiss of me to fail to mention the presence of my father in my life and its impact on my lack of trepidation concerning the awesome privilege of fatherhood. Unlike some of my contemporaries with which I grew up, fortunately my parents were together at my birth and remain together to this day. I never had to wonder if my father loved me or if my father cared because he always was there to show my brother and me an example of a real man. He provided and protected; counseled and carved out time for us so that we knew that we mattered to him. Later it would be easier for me to embrace the idea of God being a heavenly Father because to me, and especially in comparison to others, I already had a heavenly father. While others may stumble in referring to God this way because of their baggage due to paternal abandonment, it only strengthened my faith at the prospect that God was an even better father than the one I had. For just as my earthy father loved us, provided, and remained present so does our God. This should reassure us because God shows God's love for us in part by walking along side us and being with us while also supplying our needs.

My father taught us that a man should not define manhood on the basis of how many women that are in love or infatuated with him but by how he handled his responsibilities. A man takes care of what he has created. A man would do whatever it takes to ensure the wellbeing of his children. On each of these counts, our God excels and provides the only perfect model of fatherhood. Our God is not a hands-off Father who simply creates and then leaves us to our own devices. God is very much involved in our lives while long ago putting into place principles and laws to govern the existence of this world. We can praise God that like a responsible father God has not abandoned us nor expected someone else to fulfil God's role. In addition God has gone to great lengths to ensure our wellbeing and the greatest demonstration of this grace is in God's sending of Jesus in time to secure our eternity. On the journey to my fatherhood with my earthly and heavenly fathers, I had great examples to whom I could look up. God not only provides material needs for us to fulfil our roles and assignments but God also places in our lives role models to demonstrate God's expectations personified.

2

THE DISHEARTENING INCORRECT DIAGNOSIS

As it likely is for others, our next step following the successful home pregnancy test was to get the pregnancy confirmed by my wife's obstetrician. The tests confirmed that my wife was indeed pregnant with our first child and we were overjoyed. There is something to be said about those times where God allows you to witness and experience something so miraculous for the first time. This fact, long with the knowledge that some couples may try for an extended period of time to get pregnant without positive results, sobered us to the privilege of the positive test result. With this context we were careful in not coming to the conclusion that God loved us so much more than others who had no previous success of conceiving. The basis of one's theology should not be rooted in comparisons to the lives of others. Just because we conceived does not mean that we were blessed to the extent that those who did not conceive were somehow cursed.

We debated about how and when we should share the news but we decided to wait until the pregnancy became more established before disclosing our good news with others. Perhaps we did not want to get their hopes up and get them excited about a pregnancy that could very well have been unviable. When the time was right we shared our good news. One could easily connect this premise with our Christian journeys in that we hesitate to share good news lest we share it prematurely. This however is not normally due to a deficit with regard to our faith in God. Believing that God can keep and cover unborn fetuses from miscarriage is not the place wherein we struggle. Our struggle lies with wondering if God will intervene to save babies from miscarriage even with the assurance of physicians that miscarriage often is due to the body purging itself of unviable pregnancies. One of life's greatest sources of consternation and anxiety lies within the will of God as opposed to the power or ability of God. God has the power to intervene in any situation and make it turn out the way we desire but sometimes God's will leads God's power in another direction. We need to seek peace and understanding in those times where God does refuse to intervene and decides against putting God's power on display.

But how do we go on when God's failure to intervene in our circumstance leads to our suffering? How should we respond when miscarriage and other undeserved spells of suffering befall us? In what way can we explain our stubborn faith in a God who allows these things to happen especially when people expect us to be people who are strong in faith who should not interrogate God? These are all valid questions that arise out of our suffering. But the good news is that even in the bad times God is still right by our side. We cannot judge God's closeness to us based on how rough our life becomes because God is there all the time. It takes the rough times for us to really notice and appreciate God's presence.

Fortunately, our first pregnancy did not end in miscarriage as would a miscarriage between our third and fourth children. There was, however, nothing within us that made us deserve to welcome our first child as opposed to suffering the heartbreak of miscarriage. We have to be careful, especially when it comes to encouraging or ministering to others, that we do not try to draw a direct connection between our circumstances and our relationship with God. Bad things happen to us all especially those who have devoted their lives to an invisible God. God would keep us through the miscarriage we suffered but in the face of disappointment God's presence comforted us. Long before this miscarriage, with our first pregnancy, we simply would not allow ourselves to think about the possibility that we would lose this child. Worrying over things outside of our control does nothing to help us but may dishonor the God we say we trust. When God delivered us from various things God already did the hard stuff and the heavy lifting so surely God can handle what worries us now. Instead of focusing on the negative, we were overjoyed as we moved closer to telling our parents our good news.

THE DISHEARTENING INCORRECT DIAGNOSIS

One afternoon we visited my parents and talked with them for a little while about which I cannot remember. I do remember, however, that we sat in the living room close to the kitchen where my father was either cooking or cleaning. Weeks before this day had come, my wife discussed with me the desire to go with some of the women in our family to go see The Color Purple on Broadway in New York. The trip was scheduled to take place around the time when our first child, Brenton, was to be born on October 7, 2006. As we began to leave, Tanesha told my mother that she would be unable to go on the trip and blamed me for this. When given the chance to explain I told my mother that the child was only going to be a month old and I did not want Tanesha that far away. Confusion covered my mother's face as she asked repeatedly "what child?" Then Tanesha dropped the bomb and said "Ms. Pam, I'm six weeks pregnant." My mother screamed with joy after hearing the news. Such is the case when God delivered unexpected but wonderful news about our future. Perhaps the best blessings, are those that we could not see coming.

With regard to the timing, in this story we can see how we may have plans and intentions but God knows how to interrupt our plans with something better than we had planned for ourselves. The magnitude of God's gifts overshadow anything that we could fathom for ourselves. This means that sometimes we need to let God be God and check with God to make sure we are not shortchanging ourselves with our own low expectations. My mother's response was greater than I imagined. It was unrestrained and unpretentious joy without regard for her appearance or how someone may view her in a negative light. That day my mother provided a paradigm for praise. When one evaluates the greatness of God's blessing and grace, overwhelming joy flows freely as your heart is made glad. When you really consider the undeserved blessings of divinity, you will lose all regard in that moment for your personal dignity. My mother honestly expressed how she felt in that moment and demonstrated that especially with heightened emotions we need to be open, honest and transparent with God.

One day, however, a misdiagnosis dealt our hopes a temporary yet painful blow. It seems that one could only anticipate that after a mountaintop experience one has to come face to face with the valley. Even those in relationship with God have the same testimony but we should remember that the same God

THE DISHEARTENING INCORRECT DIAGNOSIS 19

who met us on the mountain will walk beside us and give us light even in the darkest of valleys. Upon confirming Tanesha's pregnancy her doctor performed a sonogram. Her physician, at the time elderly and approaching the end of his practice, incorrectly calculated her gestation and so performed a sonogram long before necessary and even before an amniotic sac would be visible. In short her doctor made a mistake; a mistake that would cost us profound emotional grief. We should realize that like this physician all of us have a season to operate in our areas of giftedness and there comes a time when we will have to step away lest we make mistakes and bring grief to undeserving persons. In health care and soul care we can cause a great deal of damage when we fail to see that our time has passed.

    The source of our grief was his assumption that due to the fact that Tanesha was pregnant and given the fact that he could not view a sac he came to the conclusion that the pregnancy must be ectopic. This means that the fertilized egg is stuck in the fallopian tube where it could not survive. It would also mean that it would have to be aborted so that it would not cause permanent damage or death. In other words, he told us that the positive tests had given us false hope.

He told us that the baby we were now anticipating was never coming. How should you respond when told the possibility with which you were pregnant must be aborted to save your life? What do you do when you feel like God has answered your prayers only to discover that you had false hope? Even while in relationship with God it is possible to lose that for which you hoped and believed was just a matter of time before it would become yours. Nothing really prepares you for such a moment. Perhaps the chief consolation is that when mourning replaces joy and dread overwhelms one's expectations we need to remember that God is still right there. Even while we are suffering, God is right there.

    Before leaving, my wife's doctor gave her a script to have a follow-up sonogram in a couple of weeks to confirm his diagnosis. We walked out of the office and my wife was in tears. While heartbroken myself, I reassured her that everything was going to be alright and that we should be patient and wait for the follow-up exam. It is easy to wallow in our own self-pity when we are in pain. However with God's help we can mature to the point where we realize that we do not live in isolation and realize that our pain is not the only pain that matters. God has a way of feeling with

THE DISHEARTENING INCORRECT DIAGNOSIS 21

us—not simply for us—and then reassuring us that everything is going to be all right no matter what it is that we are going through. We all should live the same way showing empathy and not simply sympathy for those who are suffering. We should be more like God in this regard. For example, if someone we know is in pain we should love them enough to endeavor to feel and understand their pain because we love them and are connected to them. Just as God loves is through our pains and after knowing all of the details so should we love others enough to love them through their hurts.

For our lives, getting to that next appointment seemed like it took forever. Even in the face of uncertainty we did not allow ourselves to be overwhelmed with fear instead choosing to trust God in prayer. When confronted with issues we cannot control or handle we need to have the maturity to trust God with it and believe that one way or another God is going to make it all right. As we prepared for the final verdict from the follow up, I remember parking the car and taking the long walk from the car to the building. Waiting to be seen seemed like torture. Imagine waiting to hear a second opinion on whether your hope is lost. Consider suffering silently while anticipating hearing from someone who may tell you that it is over. The good news is that we prayed sincerely and pressed forward and faced our diagnosis with courage believing God for the best but also believing in God's keeping power if we heard the worst. However, at unquestionably the darkest time in our young marriage there was a flicker of light.

In that examination room the tech applied the jelly to my wife' abdomen and looked for a sac. There it was. The sack that would house our baby was right where it should have been and the correct size for her gestation. My wife had been misdiagnosed with an ectopic pregnancy. Suddenly all the darkness that surrounded us due to this misdiagnosis was lifted and replaced with relief and renewed hope for a healthy baby on October 7. Sometimes in life people who mean well will misdiagnose you based on the inability to see what is expected. But to God be the glory that God is able to get us the correct diagnosis and fix the damage done by the misdiagnosis. God has the last word. This lesson also taught us not to place more faith in flawed individuals than we do in the perfect God who is still with us. While God works through others, God is still God! We had been blessed with the resources to investigate the initial diagnosis and were able to leave that appointment with hope and in peace due to the words of this technician. Even as a preacher it still amazes me when it comes to the power of words. For I have learned throughout my days that God knows exactly what to say in moments of great distress to make us have peace in spite of coming out of a storm.

Our prayers and our faith that fueled them were vindicated because one way or another God made it alright. We refused to embrace the diagnosis because we sought a second opinion from another professional. God heard our prayers as we prayed that the doctor and the initial diagnosis was wrong. Recognizing that even doctors make mistakes we made our requests known to God who makes no mistakes. We did not pray as if the previous diagnosis did not exist, but our prayers expressed our faith that God could make it alright and God did. We were honest with God about our fears even while exercising this activity of faith. God knows all and so God does not need us to sugarcoat how we feel. Instead God expects blunt honesty from us and gives us a freedom to fuss at God as necessary. When you honestly and sincerely place your supplications at the feet of God,

God hears them and we are witnesses that God can make everything alright.

Needless to say that when we heard that Tanesha's doctor had misdiagnosed her with an ectopic pregnancy we made the decision to choose another obstetrician; and this obstetrician has delivered all four of our children. This physician happened to be the daughter of Tanesha's old physician who soon after this misdiagnosis retired. This teaches us a number of things. Some people in our lives are seasonal and may be granted access up to a certain period of time after which they need to be replaced. Grief, disappointment, and anger are some of the potential side effects of keeping certain people in your life for too long. It reminds me of hair products in that if kept in for the right amount of time it performs as advertised but if you fail to rinse it out on time it will burn your scalp. Some of the suffering we endure is the result of keeping people in our lives for years that were only meant to remain for a season. The other thing that this teaches us is that we need to do what we can for God while we are able but then be honest and sensitive enough to the voice of God to know when it is time to turn things over to someone else.

THE DISHEARTENING INCORRECT DIAGNOSIS

Perhaps you believed yourself to be what Jonathan Nelson calls being pregnant with possibilities and it seems that miscarriage is certain. Have you ever been pregnant with something and been told that it was over before you could wrap your head around the fact that it began? Do not allow what others have diagnosed to make you lose hope and trust in God. Even though it may seem hopeless do not abandon the hopes of birthing what God has placed in you. Nobody knows your capacity like God and nobody knows the specifics of your situation like God. When the prognosis of your pregnancy is uncertain turn to God who may end up telling you that your diagnosis was incorrect. But you may never know if you do not refer your condition to a specialist or the God who specializes in doing the impossible.

3

THE MISTAKEN GENDER PREDICTION

By the time my wife Tanesha conceived, my older brother Reggie had three daughters. This coupled with the fact that my only paternal uncle did not have a son which meant that the lineage of the Meade name could be in jeopardy. Therefore, my uncle put pressure on me to have a son so that one day the Meade family name would continue. Surely there are others in similar positions where the pressure may be similar based on the hopes that you will accomplish what others around you or who have come before you have not. For some this may be graduating college or rising out of poverty among other challenges. While just as it seemed that the odds were against the continuation of our family name God had other plans. God is indeed able to bless you differently than those around you. This does not make your blessings superior or their faith and relationship with God inferior. I cannot state for certain why my first child was a son but I give glory to God for the outcome.

The time surrounding the conception of this first child lacked the sense of social and racial unrest that exists at this time of writing. This child was conceived prior to the election and inauguration of President Barack Obama, the country's first black president. The years that followed his ascension to the peak of politics have been filled with more open racial hostility than I could remember from my earlier years. The countless young black men incarcerated through a new system of oppression defined in Michelle Alexander's book *The New Jim Crow*, the seemingly innumerable lives of black males lost at the hands of police officers, and the senseless murders of black males perpetrated by others black males has made this a dangerous time to raise my son

One could believe that such odds against a son's survival would make us hesitate to even want a son. But history and theology have taught me that regardless of the circumstances in which a child is born and raised God still has a plan for that child's life. This would not be the first time that a son would be born in less than desirable times. We can look at the story of Moses who according to Exodus was born at a time of Pharaoh-ordered genocide of Hebrew males as a means to control their population. Moses' story shows us that even when someone is born in the crosshairs or comes forth into a world with a target on his or her back God still has a plan for his or her life. With God there is no set of circumstances that we are unable to overcome.

But on the other hand, it reminds me of Jesus' story. I do not suggest that my son is a savior but that just like Jesus my son was born into a tumultuous world while possessing a father who only wanted what was best. God's timing is indeed immaculate and this reminds us that God knows when the world would need your presence most. In the fullness of time, or when the time was just right, God sent Jesus. God has likewise sent each of us here for such a time as this. Brenton's story teaches that you do not have to be here long to make a significant impact. This book exemplifies the fact that Brenton already has a story. What is yours? Before we leave this earth to greet eternity with expectation, we need to deposit into those we leave behind—some type of impact that reminds our survivors that we made a difference. That is the legacy of Christ and the legacy of the Christian should be no different.

As mentioned previously, I always wanted my first child to be a son. However, regardless of my desire I knew then and now that such things are not simply a matter of preference. Scientific tinkering aside, the biological process actually determines gender. In other words, while I wanted a son I effectively understood that such a fate was out of my hands. I had a particular desire but I was powerless to call it into reality but through the grace of God we were given this son. Life is filled with moments where we are incapable of obtaining for ourselves our hearts desires but in these moments we should put our trust in God. God's grace has proven capable of providing us with better than we can imagine for ourselves.

In the weeks that followed our initial sonogram and diagnosis, peace concerning our firstborn's gender evaded me. Even as a preacher somehow, I failed to heed Ephesians 4:6 and simply ask God for what I wanted and then trust God while my heart and mind were being kept by God's grace. In spite of my anxiety on the subject, it helped to know that at twenty weeks we would be able to discover if my prayer was answered. We filled the time in between initial diagnosis and this appointment at twenty weeks by tossing around potential names for our child. In hindsight one can understand that it takes faith to put a name on one's not-yet. It is one thing to hope but another thing altogether to have so much hope and expectation that you begin to name that which has not arrived.

Finally, the day had arrived where we would learn the gender of our unborn firstborn. Once again, it felt as if we waited forever to be called back at the radiology practice. We had come principally to find out the baby's gender but also to see our child in the womb and hear about the baby's wellbeing. The tech entered the room, put the jelly on my wife's stomach, and began looking for the baby which she found quickly. She conducted measurements of the various parts of the body; measurements which would be part of the final report. As it was with my wife, it behooves us to periodically have a checkup with the

Eternal who can see through our layers and help us see the state of that with which we are pregnant. We need God to check over us periodically to make sure that the possibilities in us are properly being nurtured and growing in a way consistent with expectations. Just like in pregnancy, God may call to our attention some issues what require intervention to avoid heartbreak and disappointment.

To our relief, the tech expressed no reservations about what she observed when conducting measurements. After collecting all of the necessary measurements she asked if we desired to know the gender of our baby. We went into the appointment completely in agreement that we wanted to know the gender. The tech moved the instrument around Tanesha's stomach and asked what we wanted to which we said "a boy." She said something to the effect of "sorry, it's a girl." Knowing our expectations and hopes, I am sure she felt a sense of disappointment for us in that we were not getting what we wanted. This uneasiness has to be a part of the job of anyone whose responsibility it is to sometimes furnish unwanted "bad" news. In a way it reminds me of the prophets and even of those of us today who seek to preach prophetically knowing that sometimes the news that God calls us to share is bad news. When we hear that God is not going to do what we want or that our reality will contradict our expectations it can be disheartening for both the hearer and the speaker.

In any situation of disappointment confusion may abound concerning the source of disappointment. Am I disappointed in myself for not doing something more or for sending the wrong chromosome that resulted in the conception of a daughter? Does my disappointment lie with my wife with whom I partnered to conceive this child? Or is the source of my frustration with my God whom I served faithfully and who knew very well of my desire for a son? In life's disappointments we are tempted to cast blame to one or a combination of these three sources. If we are honest, sometimes we doubt ourselves and have low self-esteem. In others, we may doubt the veracity or integrity of those with whom we partner and think that maybe they dragged us down with them. But still in others, we may blame God for having the power to give us what we ask but choosing not to intervene to guarantee the results.

As it might be the case with you when you are in similar circumstances of disappointment, my disappointment did not stem from either of these three but rather from the situation. Life can be disappointing and yet no one is to blame. In such times it would help us to remember that disappointments happen to all of us, and that we should shift our focus to God who even in the midst of disappointment finds a way to shatter our expectations. For sometimes we are disappointed with that for which we have settled not knowing that in God's greater plan God has something greater than our expectations. For example, there were times when I desired to be with certain women and became disappointed when the relationships did not work out. I did not blame myself or my romantic interest nor did I blame God. But in the place of my disappointment God met me with a woman (my wife) who was greater than my expectations. In that moment, in the examination room, I believed that God would do the same with my firstborn child no matter the child's gender.

Initially desiring boys and a girl, our posture quickly switched from disappointment to joy knowing that our baby was healthy in spite of being told that the baby was a girl. Dealing with disappointment can be difficult especially when considering the magnitude of expectations and pressures we experience with regard to things turning out a certain way. In my experience, walking with God disappointment seems to reappear more often than I would like. In this I believe that I am not alone. Based upon our faith in God we often have lofty expectations for how our lives should be only to discover that our reality runs contrary to our ideal. My hope is that by discussing my own disappointment we can learn not to diminish our expectations of God but to be sober in knowing that life is not a fairytale. Worse than being disappointed is not possessing enough faith to expect great things from a great God. In other words, while our lives may not be as we pictured them from time to time, we can have joy based upon how well things are with the caveat that with God things can get even better.

As soon as I began to accept what this technician told me, she exclaimed "wait a minute, what is that?" At this moment it became clear that she made a mistake; it was a boy! This is twice in the process of having our first child that healthcare officials affected our emotions with misdiagnoses. Nevertheless, I grew even happier and rejoiced the more knowing that this child was a son just like we wanted. The least anyone can do when you perceive that God has blessed you with your heart's desire is to offer God praise and thanksgiving. To this day, my wife and I retell that story and recall the emotion we felt in that moment. No matter what another flawed individual pronounces over you or determines about your condition, we should always know that God has the last say.

Nothing really prepares you for the emotional rollercoaster that comes with having dreams, having those dreams dashed, and then told your dream is going to be a reality. Oftentimes we may feel pressured to accept our fate and accept the disappointment that comes along with it when life dashes our dreams. But it could be that our dreams are simply delayed as opposed to denied. In our walk with God, God may allow some of our dreams to be deferred but we ought not to lose all hope because God is able to make the faintest of dreams come true. Only with God can dreams consistent with God's character come to reality. This episode also demonstrates how quickly life can turn especially if it involves a health care professional and an incorrect diagnosis or prediction.

Most expect health care professionals to make predictions and prognostications based upon the evidence that they can observe. These professionals then expect their patients to trust them with the diagnosis of their condition of existence on faith based on the evidence the professional has reviewed. We put our wellbeing in the hands of such physicians trusting that they will do what is best for us given the information they have at the time. Our relationship with God is somewhat similar except for the fact that God is a great physician who has all of the information. As a result, we ought not to have the same sense of anxiety when it comes to trusting our lives to the capable hands of God. God always has our best interests at heart and knows exactly what to do in every situation. For just like many of us are not physicians, we cannot always see what God sees but with faith we place our belief and trust in God who we cannot see with that which we can see.

This is the message of the Christ event or his advent. We cannot readily observe the sin that contaminates our existence but God knowing the condition as well as the cure prescribed for God's Son to visit with us so that we could be saved. To accept salvation we need to trust God's diagnosis; not that we are depraved and the most vile of God's creation but that we are "fearfully and wonderfully made" but require God's treatment to be at our best. One could argue that accepting salvation is to place oneself in God's hands believing and trusting that God is going to do what is in that person's best interest. God is worthy of our trust considering that God is in position to help is, that God has the power to help us, and that God knows exactly how to affect it all. Praise God when predictions turn out to be wrong and as a result dreams come true. Given the opportunity to predict the outcome of our lives, some would no doubt have cast doubt on our success but instead of trying to fashion a label for such folks we should praise God that their prediction was mistaken.

4

Preparing for Brenton's Arrival

In the months that followed our receipt of the good news that our firstborn child would be a son my wife and I spent time getting prepared for his arrival and researching baby names. The former included setting up registries so that friends and family could purchase items that we needed for the baby. We took our best guess with regard to the items we thought we would need but failed to ask other parents about which items were truly necessary. We purchased or scanned into our registry numerous items that seemed helpful at first but in practice turned out to be a disaster. In general, we obtained items that we did not need based on their appearance without regard for practical application. This is the same sort of thinking that has infected some Christians—the idea of seeking after things that are not needed. In such cases, our eyes get us into trouble by leading us to commit our bodies or our resources to things that at their best will not help us and at their worst can harm us. Solely possessing that which we need should not be viewed as a negative especially in God's economy for our needs are all that we were promised to possess by God's provision (Philippians 4:19).

Perhaps in our case pride got in the way. This is no different than when we in times of new experiences or distress possess too much pride. This pride prevents us from reaching out to those who have already experienced and arisen from the uncomfortable and challenging place in which we find ourselves. God has blessed us and surrounded each of us with persons, many or all of whom can help us navigate through life's rough seas after already surviving them. On the other hand, we need to be transparent about the situations that God has delivered us from so that those with whom we interact and are in relationship with can reach out to us for wise counsel at the appropriate time. We should not allow pride to keep us from reaching out and from transparently extending a hand. Helping each other is one of the divinely assigned roles for us as we live in community.

As mentioned previously, in addition to acquiring the necessary resources for our baby's arrival, my wife and I also discussed and debated appropriate names for our firstborn son. One of the names that always seemed to resonate with my wife was the name that we eventually chose—Brenton. At the time, I was not fond of the name for which reasons I cannot remember. However, I was adamant that I did not want my son to become my namesake if for no other reason than that to be named after me would have been too much pressure for the boy. We did however agree that my son should take my middle name as a means to connect us and we repeated this behavior with our three daughters who share my wife's middle name.

We decided to choose conservative names because we did not want to make our son's life more difficult by adding the prospect that he may face rejection from job opportunities because his name caused employers to turn away. Surely it is sad that a parent has to consider this but we need to accept the fact that God left some responsibilities squarely at the doorsteps of fallible humankind and expects each of us to do what is just. In other words, we have to put ourselves in the best possible position to elicit the goodwill of those who hold the decks and have the power to invite us to play the game as long as it does not involve degrading ourselves or dishonoring God. God does not always intervene in these situations that are governed by the whims of the powerful but instead sometimes God intervenes by equipping us to become empowered by both experience and higher education. Put another way we should partner with God to get where we want to go.

The name that eventually stuck means "steep hill." At the time we had no idea how prophetic it would be to name our son this name due to the numerous challenges and medical concerns that would follow. Just before his premature arrival, I ventured with the men of my church to our annual retreat grounds. We had a very relaxing time filled with instruction, good food and fun fellowship. At the time, I was clueless that this time of retreat would function as the calm before my storm. Life then and since has taught me that sometimes God grants us periods of relaxation and reflection at key moments because only God truly knows what is coming. God not only knows how to calm us as we exit our storms, but God knows how to settle and sober us before venturing into more of life's storms. For this reason it is mandatory for me to take time for myself to reflect and rest so that I am better equipped to weather life's storms.

Upon arriving home, I ventured to the top floor of our four-level townhome and greeted my wife just shy of two weeks after celebrating our first anniversary as husband and wife. God granted me a time of rest and had in those weeks prior blessed my wife and me with more intimate times as part of God's plan to insulate us from circumstances that could have understandably torn us apart. God provides us with occasions where we can spend intimate time with those whom we love and with those whom God has chosen to ornament our lives prior to storms as a reminder that we are not alone. These persons with whom we share so much become like pastoral care givers and provide visible manifestations of God's invisible presence and grace. To discount their influence and to take them for granted is to dishonor the God who chose these people to be in our lives during seasons of challenge.

PREPARING FOR BRENTON'S ARRIVAL

Just as if it were yesterday, I can still remember how I laid on our bed while reporting on the time we had during the retreat in the audience of my wife who was busying herself with her hair in the bathroom. Then she called me by my name as she rarely does. My wife normally just says "hey" or starts talking with the expectation that I will know that she is talking to me and begin listening. Other times she calls me "dear" in a way that only she can. But this time she called me by my name only reinforcing the seriousness in her tone. She told me that then, almost three months before she was supposed to deliver, she believed that she was leaking amniotic fluid. She believed that her water broke. My wife Tanesha realized the seriousness of this situation given the importance of amniotic fluid and called out my name. Beloved there are times when the seriousness of our situation demands for us that we call our God by God's name. In such times we have no use for niceties nor for pet names with the recognition that desperation requires a call of desperation. There are also times when it seems that what God has given us is slipping away and in those times we need to call out to God without regard for dignity.

Upon hearing the news and observing the volume of liquid for myself we decided to call my wife's doctor who promptly directed us to go to the hospital. Fortunately the hospital in which we were to deliver was only five miles from our home. This short drive I am sure felt like forever as we found ourselves in familiar territory in danger of losing that which we hoped to receive. Knowing the role that amniotic fluid plays, including serving as a buffer to protect the baby, we were afraid of what would happen if we did not take this circumstance seriously. In this case, fear occupied the same space as faith. This is because the fear of circumstances does not suggest a lack of faith.

Being honest about the ramifications of what transpires can help us to take situations more seriously. That said, fear in the life of a Christian is not a negative as long as it drives you toward God. There is nothing weak or faithless about being fearful of what may come with inaction. Instead of being paralyzed by fear, we should let fear motivate us to seek God's guidance and assistance fully recognizing that God guides, assists, and heals often with the assistance of trained medical professionals. God could heal what ails you through miraculous intervention or God could endow humankind with the intellect to discover a prescription that can heal you. Either way God should be the one who gets the glory. We should not be so spiritual so as to fail to discern God's hand operating through the people before whom we stand.

After arriving at the hospital and watching my wife release enough liquid to soak absorptive material and her jeans we were sure that our suspicions were correct: that she had been leaking amniotic fluid. However, our assertions to this fact failed to persuade the nurses in triage who had the audacity to suggest that maybe the fluid was simply urine. They reminded me of the mistake many of us in ministry make by making presuppositions about what is going on with the people for whom we care without actively listening to what they are saying. At the same time, it may remind some of how others try to persuade us that the grave situations in which we find ourselves may not be as grave as we believe. One of the more hurtful things that we can do in ministry is to not take serious people's experiences. Just like our child could have been lost if no one would have taken us seriously the church has done great harm to persons by not taking their wounds and conditions seriously.

Perhaps the nurses in triage simply desired the simple diagnosis of bladder leakage to explain such fluid release. It no doubt would have been easier to address that problem instead of the complications associated with the premature loss of amniotic fluid. Rather than proceeding with an abundance of caution these triage nurses did a disservice to my wife who was in her care. The made the mistake of caring insufficiently about my wife as evidenced by their failure to take her words seriously especially given the fact that my wife is a nurse. Ultimately, they gave my wife the benefit of the doubt and administered a test to determine the nature of the fluid. In the end, the test proved our assertions: that it was amniotic fluid. We stood on what we knew and the results vindicated us. There are times in life where you have to have the courage of your convictions and stand on what you believe even if your beliefs are mocked or disregarded. When doing so, as it was in our case, we can have the assurance that ultimately it will be God who will vindicate us.

Upon verification of the fact that my wife was leaking amniotic fluid and that her fluid may have been completely depleted, my wife was admitted to the hospital for observation. The purpose of this was to ensure the safety and overall wellbeing of the baby who was now vulnerable to infection and therefore in danger. Truly, there are times when life takes a turn for the worse but in order to keep things from further deteriorating we need to be admitted into the care of persons who can care for us and that which we are about to birth. Some churches admit people into their churches under watch care because they need a church to look out for them in their season of transition. From time to time all of us need such support. Praise God that God knows how to surround us with specialists and experts who are uniquely gifted and qualified to watch after our spiritual conditions lest things deteriorate further.

Given the baby's susceptibility to infection and the fact that he was no longer surrounded by protective fluid the doctors raised the prospects of my wife having to remain on bedrest in the hospital for the remainder of her pregnancy. This way the doctors would be able to flush fluid in to the womb in order to keep the baby in the best possible condition. They had the technology and the wherewithal to make the best of the situation given their options. Oftentimes we who walk with God find ourselves in a similar position of having to use what we have to make the best of our situation. Fortunately, God gives us what we need to do just that. So instead of asking God to start over and deal us a new hand, we need to ask God for the wisdom to expertly play the cards our hand has been dealt. We need God's wisdom to make the best of life's circumstances especially when things are beyond our control.

There was nothing that my wife did to bring on this event. She was not guilty of overexerting herself bringing about the premature act of her water breaking. Rather, she took care to ensure that she did not put too much stress on her body and therefore the baby. Like many others, there was nothing she did or we do to bring about what others may call a misfortune. We are not alone in finding ourselves in the precarious position of having to wrestle with circumstances of which we were not the cause. Sometimes unfortunate things happen even to Christians. This is not because of the devil necessarily or because we make enemies of the unrighteous but because unfortunate things happen to all of us. God does not always choose to intervene to prevent such unfortunate situations but God does give us what we need to endure them. However, unrealistic expectations of God that have not been interrogated may lead us to disappointment when asking why God would intervene there and not here or then but not now. Where is God when such things occur? God is right there with us, walking beside us, and helping us to endure what some may believe is unsurmountable.

5

BRENTON ARRIVES PREMATURELY

In the hospital, we wrestled to come to grips with this sudden onset of circumstance and we could not help but feel a sense of anxiety. This was not due to some lack of faith on our part or disbelief concerning God's ability to bring us out of this with a healthy baby boy. Our anxiety stemmed from a lack of familiarity with such circumstances. At the time, I had not known any other parents who had to deal with a similar situation. Consequently, I rested on my faith so that I believed that it was not a matter of if my son was going to make it but just a matter of time before he would be out of the hospital and everything would be alright. In these moments of anxiety I remembered that according to Philippians 4:6 that I did not have to remain anxious so I prayed to God in this situation for God to bring my son out of this. Then I experienced the promise of that verse as I was overcome with the incomprehensible peace of God that would keep me from that moment until he would come home much later. If you trust God's promises and put God's directions into action I am a witness that God will come through.

Another element that helped us with our anxiety was the overwhelming loving presence of family and friends who visited us while we were in the hospital. All of those persons who were closest to me, including friends, family and my pastor came and prayed with us while blessing us with the ministry of presence. It is amazing how much of an impact it can make for those persons who are the most cherished in one's life to show up and make their presence felt especially in times of trouble. This sounds much like the God that I serve. God can intervene and bless us through the comforting presence of other people and in other ways. In all these ways God reminds us through the ministry of presence that we are not alone and that we shall overcome. In spite of being surrounded with strangers and the busyness of life it is still possible for life to become a lonely place and for it to feel as if we are walking alone. Having stated this, I praise God that in one's loneliest hours God reminds us that God is right there. Along the lines of Andrae Crouch's song "Through It All" God lets us know that we belong to him. There is no better place to be than in the hands of almighty God who is love.

Just as it seemed that we knew what the subsequent months would hold, things changed. My son suffered from self-induced distress. Not only do we believe he tried to break his way out of the womb and caused my wife's water to break, but he began grasping the umbilical cord and depriving himself of oxygen. At twenty-eight weeks gestation he did not know what he was doing and that he was harming himself. But we praise God that we were in the hospital surrounded by capable physicians and nurses who detected the distress before proceeding with what would come next. How many times have we engaged in self-destructive behavior ignorantly? Some of us are here in part because even while we ignorantly self-destructed we were surrounded with people who not only cared but who helped us by shepherding us through those times. God works through people in this way. God operates through those who are around us and who may see us going in the wrong direction. In many ways that is the message of the Cross. God saw humanity engaging in self-destructive behavior and intervened through Jesus Christ to show us that we were heading in the wrong direction. God dispatched the Balm in Gilead to heal us and show us the error of our ways. Jesus was sent to stabilize humanity's condition in part by showing us how this life should be lived.

The health care providers consistently monitored our son's condition. We were fortunate to have insurance that covered everything our son needed including the time of his caregivers. The importance of the presence of people who can help us cannot be overstated. Part of the reason we live in community is to help each other. One of the benefits to civilization is that we can look out for each other and help return those to the light who are dangerously close to being lost to the darkness. The failure of some to be surrounded by such persons may be the result of their own personal choices or the failures of others to care enough about others to invest the time to look after them. In either case, the failure does not lie with God. Just imagine the blessedness of our community if each of us were surrounded by others who not only cared about our wellbeing but who offered unique skillsets and gifts for the benefit of keeping us whole.

    Being under the watchful eye of these trained professionals could not help us to avoid what came next. My son placed himself in such distress that it became the recommendation of the doctors that they perform an emergency caesarean section to ensure the baby's survival. They wanted to cut him out, although he was twelve weeks premature, in order to keep him alive. This shows that sometimes what God is birthing from us may need to be born prematurely to keep alive what seemed fated to die in the womb. Some dreams are better off born prematurely and left to struggle in the aftermath rather than left to self-destruct in the womb of our minds. We should not be dismayed however. This is because the same God who planted the seeds of our dreams and who incubated them with our understanding that God was able to bring them to pass, can keep alive even that which was born prematurely. Perhaps this is why at that moment anxiety and worry did not overwhelm me. I believed that God was able to bring our child out just fine. In this belief, I was vindicated.

The prayers of the righteous overshadowed us as we approached the time that our son would be born: between eleven in the evening and midnight. Prior to his arrival, a health care professional gave my wife a shot of steroids for the purpose of stimulating my son's lung development before he was born. God knows exactly when and how to stimulate the growth and development of what is in us so that even after being born prematurely it can still function. God knows that providing the right kinds of opportunities and experiences that stretch us will have the added benefit of furthering the development of what God wants to birth from us. God knows how to boost what God planted in us so it can survive outside of us. Some of us may be afraid of birthing what God put in us because we are afraid that once it is outside of us it is doomed to die or fail. But the good news from Brenton's story is that God can help us and that which we birth to survive an arrival ahead of schedule.

Surgery was set and we knew that before the day was over that our son would be born. To prepare my wife for surgery, the doctors called an anesthesiologist to come and administer an epidural to my wife. An epidural is when local anesthesia is applied to the spine through an injection in the back to prevent a patient from feeling anything below the waist. This would ensure that my wife would not feel the excruciating pain of going through this surgery. Do we believe that this is the way that God sometimes works? Does God help us to get to the point that we are numb so that we do not feel the pain from the surgical procedures that God performs on us? Perhaps not to this extent. But God does administer enough anesthesia to make our process bearable so that we will not quit or sabotage our moments of deliverance. For example, God sometimes affords us the opportunity to say goodbye and spend final moments with people before they die. Such times dampen the pain of what is coming in those instances because we were able to say our peace. Like the doctors, with God's help we are able to endure the most painful of experiences because God knew the pain before the process ever started.

While completing initial surgical work on my wife, the doctors had me put on a sterile suit so that I would not introduce things to the environment that could potentially lead to an infection with my wife. The pants fit just fine while the top was a little too tight.

Nevertheless, I was clothed with garments suitable for the surgical moment. This was a requirement for me if I wanted to be in the room to witness my son being born in the world. Without it I could have contaminated the operating room and put my wife and son's lives in jeopardy. This memory helps us to see that we should not be surrounded with people who are contaminated with the wrong things and who are not properly prepared so as not to endanger us while we birth what God planted in us. People who are contaminated with negativity or doubt must be covered with pure hearts and pure motives before being allowed to witness what God is doing. People who are not willing to sacrifice their comfort for our calling do not deserve to be in the room and should therefore be disallowed. For in the moments when the destiny that God has planted in you comes forth, what you birth has to be more important than the feelings or judgments of those who want to be around you.

Stepping into the surgical room I noticed that the doctors had already begun to work on my wife. They had already sterilized the area, made an incision across her abdomen, and used what I believe to be retractors to open up the area. The doctors maneuvered in her womb to retrieve my son.

However, my wife was in a great deal of pain and so the anesthesiologist applied more local anesthesia by pouring it into the open womb. In spite of her struggles and observing the pain and pressure on her face, my wife's doctor pulled out my son twelve weeks before she had initially predicted. He was born prematurely and although undersized he was ours. Circumstances in life may lead to the premature birthing of things in our lives whether they are businesses, ministries, or other endeavors. However, the good news is that although they may come out undersized and premature according to the experts, by the grace of God, they may be strong enough to survive. When they are not strong enough to survive, just as it is with some newborns, it is not an indictment against God. Children do not live while others die because God loves one child more than another or one set of parents more than the other. We have to recognize that God knew from the beginning what was born was not going to survive. So the question is not necessarily "God why did you not intervene and save my baby?" but rather "since my baby did not survive, God help me heal and grow from this situation." This is much easier for that about which we speak metaphorically than it is about real babies. The experience is painful nonetheless.

Due to his condition when he was born, we did not get to enjoy all the normal immediate moments with the baby but instead they rushed him to the neonatal intensive care unit (NICU) where he would spend the first few weeks of his life. Joy overwhelmed me even for those few moments where I was able to lay my eyes on my son. My excitement was somewhat tempered when upon visiting him I saw all that it took to keep him alive. He had a feeding tube, breathed through a ventilator, and was covered with leads to monitor his heart and his oxygen level. He looked to be in pretty bad shape but the peace that began walking with me from the day before still remained with me and in me. As a result, I determined that it was not a matter of if he was coming home; but rather a question of when. This conviction would not waver in spite of the setbacks that he would experience in the days, weeks, and months to come. I am not suggesting that walking with God is the reason that my son survived but now I know that no matter what it looks like God stayed right there with us. The lesson learned is that God will not abandon us in spite of what happens. Even when what you believed God for and birthed with God's help remains on life support, God will be right there.

We visited him for the few days that my wife remained in the hospital but eventually we had to leave him there and return home to a house that waited for his arrival. The pain and disappointment of having to do this is unexplainable. Imagine waiting all this time for something to arrive and what arrives does not arrive in the condition you expected. Then imagine that even though it is not what you expected you are still grateful for it but have to suffer because while it has arrived it is not ready for you to take possession. Walking with God is not a guarantee that such circumstances will not come. But the good news is that while we had to leave our son behind we were not alone—God was still right there with us. Not only that but we trusted that the same God who walked with us would also remain with Brenton as his story had only begun to be written.

6

THE HOSPITAL JOURNEYS

Brenton started his journey after his birth in the neonatal intensive care unit (NICU) of Harbor Hospital in Baltimore. While we made every effort to visit him from his birth until the day of my wife's discharge, he required more weeks of treatment and monitoring so we had to leave him behind. Leaving him behind in that hospital was one of the hardest things that we ever had to do but it was made easier by our understanding that there was little we could do for him other than visit him. For while we loved him with our whole heart, what he needed we could not provide. So we left him in the capable hands of doctors and nurses at the hospital while trusting them with our son. Truly we need to mature to the point where although we love them we have to leave the ones we love in the care of our God who is more than capable of giving them what we need. Becoming overly stressed over situations that you cannot change only imperils you and raises the prospect that the ones you love will be robbed of your presence. We should let God handle those situations over which we have no control and trust God's expertise. After all, God made us all. But getting to this state of mind takes time and maturation. We should not crucify ourselves if we are not there yet. As we grow old with God and our relationship with God strengthens, it becomes easier for us to let go and let God handle those crises or problematic circumstances in which we are powerless. We can do this as we learn to quickly realizing in these moments that impossible situations for us are prime opportunities for God to show God's power.

    In spite of our best efforts, we could not completely remain free of stress. We knew that he was in the hospital and in capable hands but we also knew that to hasten the day when he could come home Brenton would need to grow and his condition had to improve. In light of this, my wife and I made it a point to call the NICU nightly to check on his status. Sometimes the news would be positive as they shared that he had taken some steps forward in his development. But other times we would call only to hear that on several occasions he had stopped breathing causing his heart rate to drop. If you recall, he had been born so prematurely that his respiratory system was not completely developed although it was mature enough for him to be born and use a ventilator.

Our concern for him weighed so heavily upon us that when we travelled with our church to Hershey Park we could not enjoy ourselves. Instead we wandered around the park for hours refusing to have fun because our hearts remained at a NICU in south Baltimore. My wife was so overwhelmed that she began to struggle with postpartum depression. Life can turn out so differently from what we expect that it takes us to a dark place due to unrealized expectations. Sometimes life overwhelms us and the dark elements seem to drown out any semblance of light but in those times we should remember that God is still with us. God's presence specializes in bringing light to the darkest of times. In my wife's darkest hour all I could do was be there for her. I imagine that it is especially hard when what you have birthed is struggling to stay alive. But I remembered about the ministry of presence. In times when those we love struggle, we need to remember to bless them with our presence knowing that many times words are unnecessary.

Normally family and friends treat expectant parents to a baby shower to give them gifts in anticipation for the baby that is coming. This practice is a reminder of how God knows how to surround us with people who are truly happy to celebrate with us. I remember going through the stores and scanning all of the things we believed that we needed for our son's arrival. We tried to prepare for a joyous birth never knowing that his birth would come so much sooner than expected. In spite of all of the ways that we attempt to prepare for what life will throw our way, through circumstances God reminds us that preparedness is relative. There are some things for which no one can sufficiently prepare. While for others this may include the death of a child, for us it was the premature birth of our son who was born so early that he preceded the shower held in his honor. There were pictures at the shower that showed

Brenton with tubes all over him. We were able to show how he was because we believed God for what he is. Those pictures were our way of celebrating him and owning his circumstance. You have to own your circumstance in order to entrust God with changing it.

Instead of celebrating in anticipation of his arrival, our friends and family celebrated after he was born with a mix of excitement and sadness given the fact that although he was here he could not attend. Their presence symbolized the invisible presence of God because through their faith they believed he was coming because otherwise they never would have purchased gifts that would torment us if we were to lose him. God knows how to place people in our lives who not only celebrate with us but who believe God with us for what God has promised us. Any friends and family can stay resolute when life is easy but it takes friends and family of faith to pray with you and stand in expectation for how God will turn things around. With them being there for us, in hindsight it is clear that Brenton's story would inspire others to believe God for the improbable. This includes my pastor who a few years after Brenton's arrival would have to watch helplessly as his grandson fought for his life. Seeing Brenton's survival only could strengthen his faith and trust in what God was able to do. Praise God for the testimonies that God blesses us to see because they remind us that there is a God somewhere. Their stories remind us that since God still reigns, a turnaround is still possible.

This leads us to consider how our struggles can prepare us for future struggle. Back in 2006, my pastor asked me to preach for the first time after Brenton was born prematurely. I remember how after the sermon my mother said that others were curious at how I would respond and preach as a result of the aftermath of the premature birth. She said that it was obvious after that sermon that I had come out of that circumstance more powerful than ever and I owe all glory to God. Sometimes God allows us to go through inconceivable difficulties because God knows that we will come out more powerful than we were when we went in. God does not allow difficult days so that they can weary us for the sake of weariness, but rather God knows how to bring the best out of us. Some of the greatest athletes are those who under the greatest of pressure knew how to rise to the occasion. God's children are no different.

In spite of the tremendous care he received at Harbor Hospital, he kept taking steps back in his development. He continued having difficulties breathing and so the doctors made the decision to transfer him to the John's Hopkins Hospital NICU. He was leaving one hospital and on his way by ambulance to a better hospital. This shows us that God knows how to take us from great to greater in order for us to get better. Whether it is a job or a relationship or something else altogether God knows how to get us from great to greater but ensuring our stability while we are in route. In other words, God knows how to take us from one place to a better place but in a way that keeps us alive in the process. At Hopkins he would have great physicians who worked at a hospital with a world-class reputation. When we entrust what we have to God's hands we can be sure that we are putting our valuables in the hands of a God who has a reputation greater than anyone else's. As it was with Brenton's new doctors, we can have confidence in God's care for what matters most to us because God's reputation speaks for itself.

Not surprisingly, Brenton's condition improved during the weeks that he lived at Hopkins. We visited him so frequently that I can still remember the exact route we would take to get there. At Hopkins, the staff allowed us to hold him and feed him. They would feed him milk that my wife pumped and froze before taking it to the hospital. Imagine that! In spite of the grief and sadness that came with having a son in the hospital, my wife still had to do her part and pump so that he would have the very best to eat so that his body could be strengthened. This shows us how God does the heavy lifting, and God partners with professionals to help us, but that God also expects us to do our part. Many may be tempted to give up or wallow in self-pity because your dreams are on life-support, but one has to ask what you are feeding your dreams. Brenton's story shows that we have a part to play in seeing our dreams come true. We need to give God something to work with and participate in our own miracles.

Even with his overall improvement, his stay at Hopkins was not without its setbacks. Brenton still had some issues that delayed his release. So while your ducks may all be in a row, you have done your part and have put yourself in the best possible position to succeed, there may still be bumps in the road. Things may not go according to plan. But in spite of his setbacks, he kept working toward getting better. This is how God would have us approach our challenges. Instead of getting discouraged and giving

THE HOSPITAL JOURNEYS

up because things do not turn out exactly the way we expected we need to keep working toward getting better. For while they are frustrating, bumps in the road remind us of some good news: we are moving forward. Eventually he improved so much that he was able to be transferred to Mt. Washington Pediatric Hospital because he no longer needed the level of care that he received at Hopkins. He was not ready to go home but he was better. God knows that sometimes we are not completely ready but I believe that God delights in us getting better. We may not be perfect in any area but we should get better.

At Mt. Washington, Brenton continued to improve so much so that we looked forward to the day when he would come home. In order to prepare him for his trip home he had to sit in his car seat to verify that sitting in the seat on the way home would not cause him any harm. The hospital wanted to make sure that he had not been alive all this time in the hospital to die on his way home. This reflects how God often treats us. God puts us through extra processes and checks so that when it is time to leave where we are, we do not die on our way to our destination. Also, the hospital required us to take a CPR class so we could learn how to administer it in case of an emergency with Brenton.

Not only will God help is in our processes but God wills that those who care for God's children receive life-saving training. For pastors and leaders this means that you have no business looking after someone else's soul while being unwilling to be trained in pastoral care and other disciplines that can help save somebody's life. We did what we had to do to prepare for him to come home and praise God he did.

7

THE LONG-AWAITED HOME ARRIVAL

One day the day came for Brenton to come home. My wife and I travelled to the hospital to pick him up. This meant that finally we would be able to do what we could only do during visits with Brenton. We would be able to hold him, talk to him, and have him look us in the eyes as he used to do in the hospital only now we would be able to do these things every day. Imagine entrusting something that you love more than life itself to someone else and then the day comes where you finally take possession. For the first time in his life he would not be in the care of doctors but in the care of his parents. This makes one think about our Heavenly Father and how one day he took possession of what matters most: our spirits. We had entrusted our spirits to other people and other things but praise God that one day we handed ourselves over to the capable hands of God. Just as we rejoiced, no doubt God rejoiced in that day where spiritually speaking we came home.

After all of the prayers uttered, agonizing calls made, and trips to hospitals taken our Brenton finally came home. God vindicated our faith that it was not a matter of if he was coming home but rather when. God will show you in drastic ways that your faith in God is not misplaced. But had the unthinkable occurred our faith in God would have remained resolute because of what we experienced months prior. Before Brenton was born, our family had to say goodbye to my cousin who passed away in his mother's womb very close to his due date. While we rejoiced on one hand, we were conflicted on the other because our family still grieved the loss of my cousin. This loss helped me to wrestle with the issue of theodicy or how bad thing still happen even while a good God rules. That circumstance showed me that

THE LONG-AWAITED HOME ARRIVAL

the circumstances may not turn out the way that we want them but God still walks beside us even when God chooses not to intervene in the way we anticipate. God intervened then to help our family heal so we could still celebrate Brenton.

I remember the ride home like it was yesterday. My wife sat in the back seat with him to keep an eye on him while I drove slower than usual. We wanted to take great care of him on his way home to make sure he was alright as he took a journey he had never taken before. For the first time he rode without being attached to wires and tubes. For the first time he would head to the only house that he has called home. God knows how to change things or how to shift things so that what you used to need, you no longer need. God knows when we are truly ready to go from our place of preparation to our place of residence. God prepares us knowing that eventually we will outgrow and lose use for the places we currently occupy. As we did with Brenton, we have to trust that God knows what is best and that God will move us when we and our destinations are ready for the move.

Family and friends blessed us with an outpouring of love after we returned home. All of the items that sat for months unused from the baby shower also served as visual reminders that they loved Brenton and us. Finally we used these items in the care of our son. That circumstance suggests that God will allow us to take possession of things we do not need now because God knows that we will need them in the future. This reminds me of my first robes that I purchased as an associate minister. Long before I earned my doctorate degree I ordered robes with doctor bars stitched on the sleeves. This I did because I liked the way that they looked. God graces us with clothes we are not fit to wear, because God knows that one day those clothes will fit. God always sees the big picture even when we are short-sighted.

We were relieved after he finally came home but he still required special care. The hospital sent him home knowing that there could be short-term and long-term consequences of his premature birth especially when it came to his lungs. They knew that he may still stop breathing from time to time so they sent us home with an apnea monitor. This device, using leads placed on his chest, would make an extremely loud noise if he stopped breathing and caused his heart rate to drop. On several occasions in the first few months after his arrival at home Brenton stopped breathing oftentimes waking us out of our sleep. Although those moments scared us, we were grateful that we had the machine so that we could know when we needed to nudge him into breathing. This reminds me of the times in life when God will cause some alarms to go off in our lives to alert us to the fact that something is wrong. Praise God also for the safeguards that God puts in place so that we can alert God to the fact that we recognize we need God to come to our rescue.

In the early days Brenton also struggled with gastric reflux that put him in a great deal of pain. So we had to thicken his formula to make sure that the formula stayed in his stomach. In other words we had to add more substance to the formula so that it could properly benefit him. Perhaps this parallels why so many Christians are malnourished in the churches that they attend. In this age many preachers have provided churchgoers with a steady diet of shallow sermons that lack the substance necessary to give them what they need to keep fighting and striving through the week. Instead of believing that good meat makes its own gravy, preachers have taken a path that has led to them producing messages that boost the ego but do nothing for the soul. God wants us properly nourished so the greater the substance within a sermon the more difficult it will be for its hearers to expel. As it was with Brenton's doctors, God knows what we need in order for us to get where God wants us to be.

In addition to all of Brenton's difficulties, Brenton also had a steep hill to climb when it came to his physical and mental development. Due to the fact that he was born prematurely, Brenton had to work hard to catch up to the normal benchmarks for his age. A nurse visited with us to check on Brenton's wellbeing. Also, since he was a preemie, he became eligible to participate in the Infants and Toddlers program that helps children catch up developmentally. These people blessed our lives through how they worked diligently with Brenton. If Brenton's testimony is any indication, God knows how to bless us by putting people in our lives who can help us overcome the challenges that life throws our way. Again, Brenton did not ask to be born prematurely and we often do not ask to be placed in difficult circumstances but God always has the last word as to how things will play out. These people reminded me of God's persistent presence in our lives and how God does not always intervene to stop unfortunate things from happening but will see about God's children and help them to overcome the fallout.

THE LONG-AWAITED HOME ARRIVAL

By the grace of God, over the course of months Brenton caught up to other kids his age when it came to his mental and physical development. This shows that even if life deals you a bad hand, with God it is still possible to win. Even if life deals you a setback, God can give you what you need to catch up to everyone else and in some cases to surpass others. Maybe you started late in life with your education, or it has taken you longer to get married and have a family, but whatever the case is God is able to help us catch up according to God's will. God can help us to discern whether or not our goals are unrealistic as we continue to believe that with God nothing is impossible.

In January, 2008 we welcomed our second child whose arrival in many ways contrasted Brenton's arrival. Our daughter Brielle arrived on schedule on a warmer than usual January afternoon. She was born without difficulty or controversy. She required no extra attention in her early development. Brielle came home with us two days after she was born. This was the good news. However, her arrival caused problems for her older brother who was then eighteen months old. He wanted nothing to do with her and acted out because he did not want her there. In those days instead of medical care or exercises to catch him up with others, Brenton needed special attention. He needed us to care for his emotions to ensure him that we had not forgotten him. In other words, Brenton alerted us to a problem and by doing so he gave us the chance to fix the problem. This sounds, in a way, like prayer and how when need something from God, God wants us to make God aware of what we need. This is not because God is ignorant of what we need, but it demonstrates that we trust God with it and believe that God is able to do something about it.

Not only did Brenton catch his peers, but he was able to successfully begin school at the age of two. He struggled with some physical activities, such as cutting with scissors, but for the most part he kept pace with the other students and improved by the end of the school year. In the years since, periodically Brenton has struggled with other health issues such as asthma, a curve in his spine, tonsils that had to be removed, and allergic reactions but he has survived. In spite of all that he has already been through, Brenton survived and is a testimony of what God can do. Through faith and with the support of others, we weathered the storms of his early years and he has come out of all those things a strong, smart, and gifted young man. As my father likes to say, in this "God has earned the right to be praised."

8

THE BRENTON WE KNOW NOW

Brenton thrived in the years that followed his initial struggles. In spite of seasonal and temporary struggles with asthma related issues, he has been physically active in sports. This means that in spite of the hand that life dealt him, Brenton did not let his struggles nor his setbacks keep him from doing what he wanted to do. God allows us each to go through our own set of struggles but rather than using our struggle as an excuse we should praise God that we survived. This should also motivate us to keep going no matter what difficulties lie on the horizon believing that the same God who helped us then can still help us now.

Not only has Brenton excelled physically but he is now a bright and talented musician who plays three instruments. He took piano lessons for years since the age of four and even competed in school competitions before serving as the minister of music for our Sunday school devotionals. He also quickly learned how to play the violin and became a top rated violinist in his grade toward the end of third grade. This year he started to play the flute out of his desire to play in the band. No one could accuse him of failing to try and utilize the gifts that God has given him. But what about us? God graciously provided each of us with our own gifts and talents that we should use to uplift God's kingdom and to be a blessing to others. Brenton is a reminder of the fact that none of us should close our eyes and greet eternity without using the gifts that God has given us to make a difference.

A naturally gifted musician, Brenton still had to take lessons, learn from his instructors in school, and practice for hours on end to become as great as he is. As it was with Brenton, God places people in our lives who can help us to develop our gifts in order to maximize our gifts' impact. So no matter how much you may be gifted, part of demonstrating gratitude for that gift is in the work we put in to sharpen our gift. This means seeking appropriate training and development while also trusting God to bless us in our efforts while believing God for greater results. We believed in Brenton's ability to play the piano, along with his sister Brielle, to the extent that we purchased a piano on which he could practice. We invested in his gifts just as God does the same for us. God mobilizes resources to help us develop and strengthen our gifts because God sees potential in us and loves us. But we also must remember that just as we invested in Brenton's gifts, God expects us to invest in our own.

While excelling in musicianship, Brenton also excelled in the classroom. Even though he currently is in the fourth grade he already earned straight A's many times including all year in second grade and twice last year. When focused he is a model student both academically and in his behavior. Brenton only earned these grades because of his ability to focus and be intentional about achieving his goals. The same could be said of what God wants from each of us when it comes to our success and achieving our goals.

We need to focus on doing our very best with what God has given us and be intentional about being successful.

When he was in the hospital, I told him that we had high standards in our house. In other words, I told him that even though he started out behind and with many difficulties we believed that he had the DNA to be successful without excuse. We believed in him long before he would pick up a pencil or attend his first class. Similarly, God knows that we are capable of succeeding because God knows what we are made of considering that God is the One who made us. As it is with Brenton, we are without excuse for not doing the best we can with what we have. We told Brenton long ago that while we had high expectations, we would only be disappointed in him if he did not try his best. I believe the same to be true of God. In other words, I believe that God is disappointed when we do not try or fail to give our best.

Outside of his musical talents and academia, Brenton also has strived to be a model Christian. He accepted Christ as his Savior and I had the privilege of baptizing him. His commitment to Christ was not confined to the altar but instead he joined the youth choir and the junior ushers while also being an active participant in Sunday school. He shows that salvation is not about coming down the aisle just to have a license to be saved and do nothing. His story shows that we are not simply saved from something but also saved to do something more. God wants each of us to seek God to discover where we fit in the Kingdom's puzzle so that we can make the greatest impact. Each of us should seek God to discover our purpose so that we can walk in our calling. God saved us for such a time as this in order to make an impact. What has God put you here to do? Unless you can answer this question, hearing "well done" one day may be elusive.

In our time raising Brenton we have not been perfect and we have made our share of mistakes. But we believe that God helped us to be there for Brenton each step of the way. We believe that having someone you love and trust on your side does wonders for your self-confidence. This is the type of reassurance that God's presence provides us. Even though we cannot see God, God is right there just like we were with Brenton. This is true except for the fact that God can be there for us wherever we are whereas we were limited where Brenton was concerned. Knowing that God is there and on our side should give us all the confidence in the world that there is nothing that we cannot accomplish. There is no obstacle too great to overcome. There exists no enemy too powerful for our God. If Brenton's story is any indication, the best is truly yet to come. If Brenton's story teaches us anything, it is that with God we can overcome anything and excel at the same time.

THE PICTURES

THE PICTURES

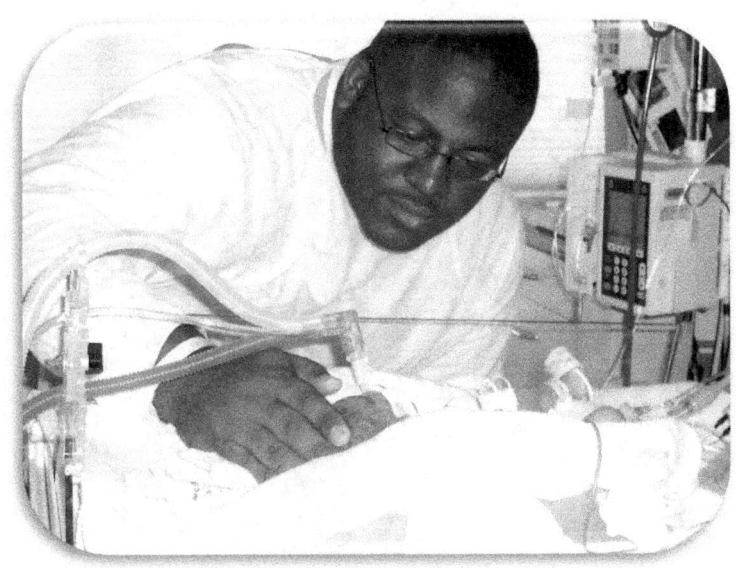

1 Day Old

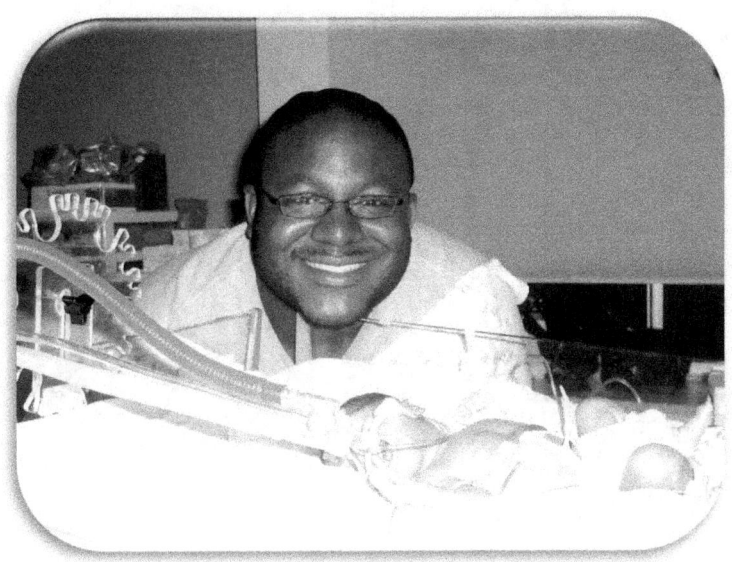

1 Week Old

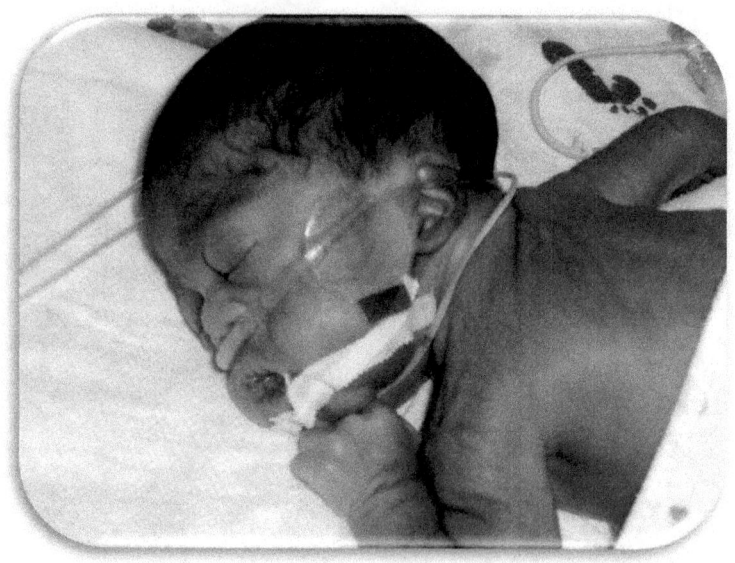

2 Weeks Old

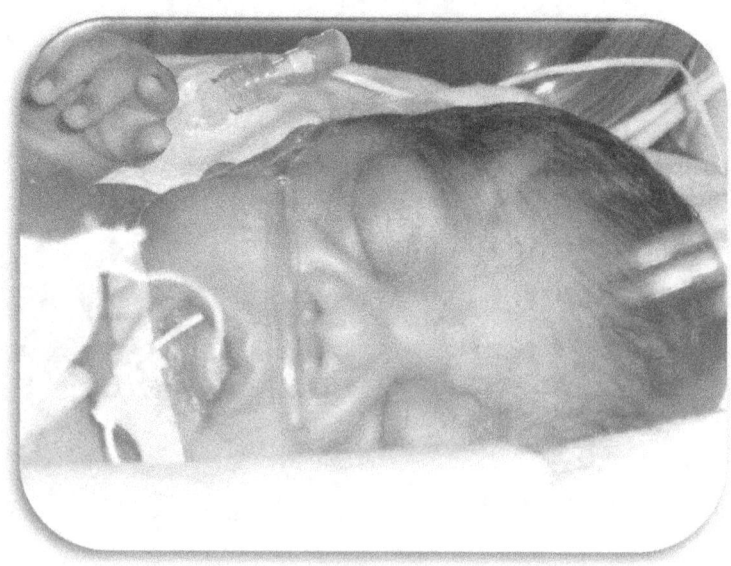

3 Weeks Old

THE PICTURES

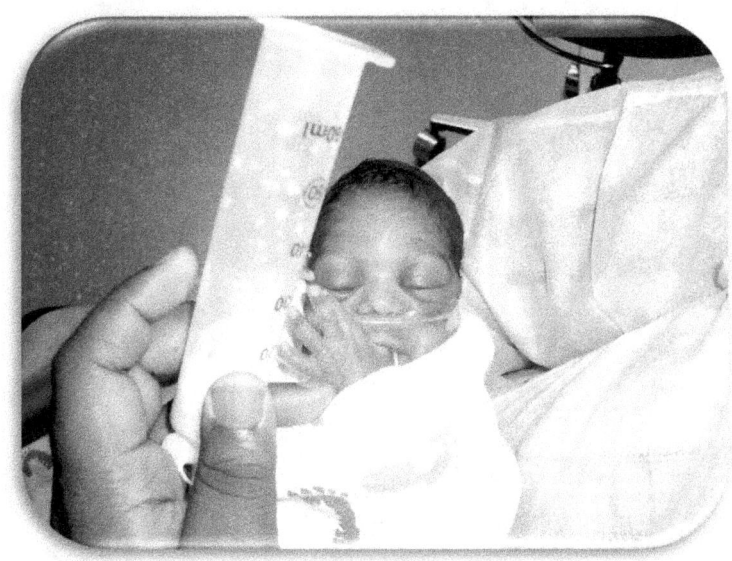

4 Weeks Old

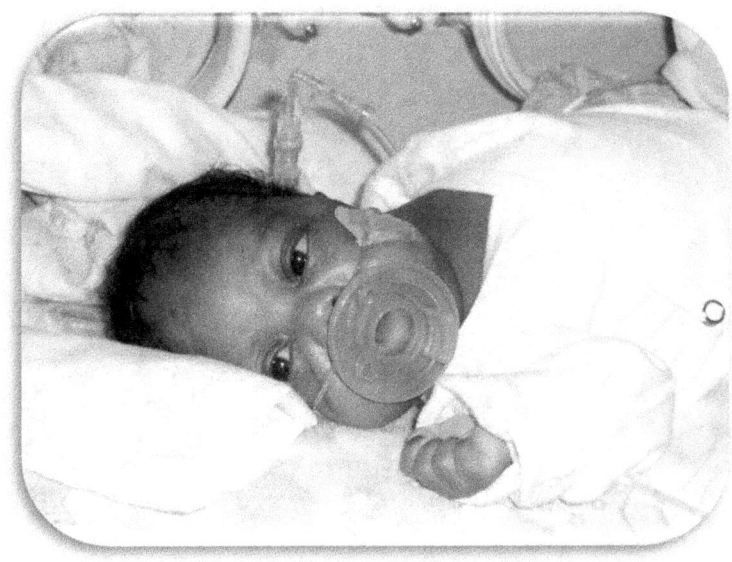

2 Months Old

3 Months Old

6 Months Old with his Mom

THE PICTURES

1 Year Old

2 Years Old

3 Years Old with baby sister Brielle

4 Years Old with Mom & baby sister Brielle

THE PICTURES

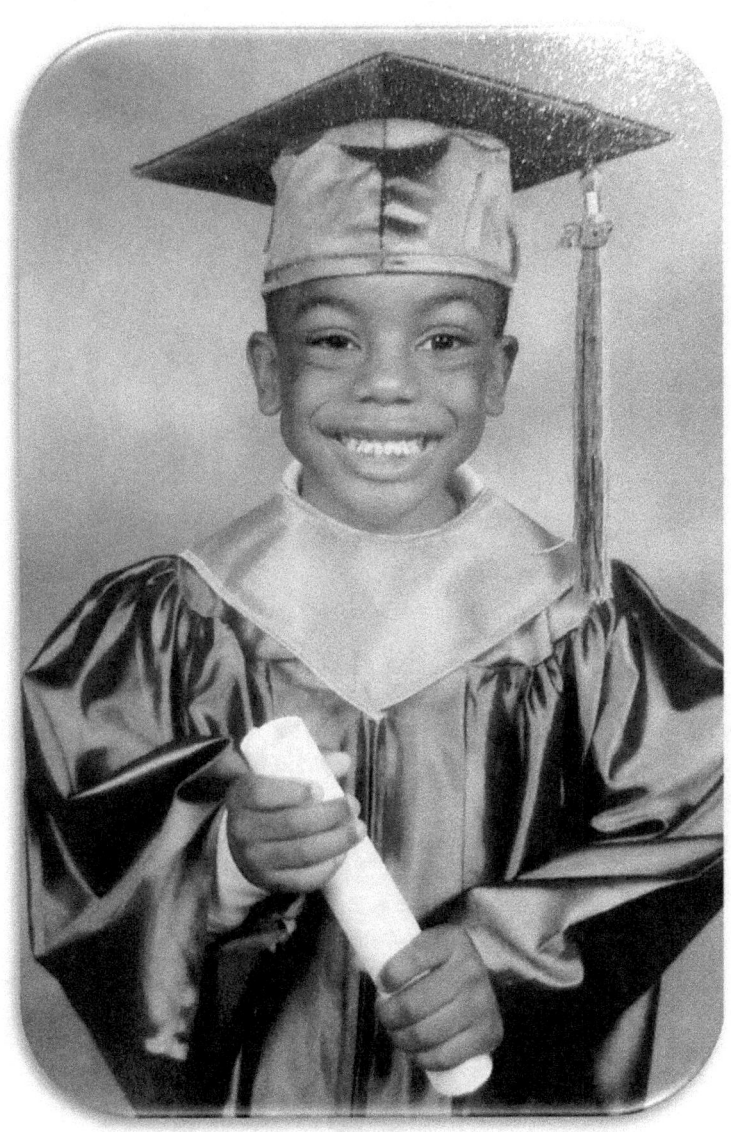

5 Years Old

6 Years Old

7 Years Old with baby sister Braeyen

THE PICTURES

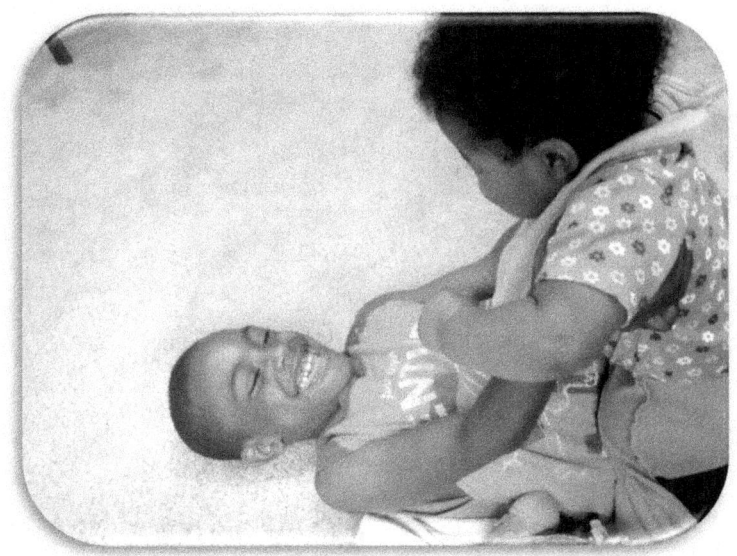

8 Years Old with baby sister Brooklan

9 Years Old

Present Day

www.ingramcontent.com/pod-product-compliance
Lightning Source LLC
Chambersburg PA
CBHW050601300426
44112CB00013B/2018